# A MOMENT OF SKY!

## Poetry with Space to Write

### BILL LEMMER

Copyright 2017 Bill Lemmer

Published 2017.

Cover illustration of the author by Christopher Munday, jacket design by Triangle Design.

All rights reserved. No part of this book may be reproduced or transmitted in any form or by any means, electronic or mechanical, including photocopying, recording, or by any information storage and retrieval system without the written permission of the author, except where permitted by law.

This book is a work of fiction. Names, characters, places, and incidents either are products of the author's imagination or are used fictitiously. Any resemblance to actual persons, living or dead, events, or locales is entirely coincidental.

First printing: 2017.

ISBN-13: 978-0-9933370-4-8

British Cataloguing Publication Data

A catalogue record of this book is available from The British Library.

These poems are for family and friends and untold others skinned to sun lit lands everywhere curling care for each other through nearest flesh yearning like everyone for joy in living under milked skies.

B.L.

## A MOMENT OF SKY!

is a writing in book for full hearts to find vent
on lined pages alongside these poems
dissolving as you put pen to paper,
a conduit of lively reading
evoking personal awareness
thoughts-feelings-memories-sensations
trawling the mouth hole of these poems,
ongoing living voices:
writing alters everything.

A Note from the Author
AMomentofSky@gmail.com

# CONTENTS

| | |
|---|---|
| A Moment of Sky! | 9 |
| Inside Wally's Wagon Wheel  (A Small Café) | 11 |
| Mercantile Solace | 13 |
| Life's Most Recent Day  is a Picnic with Friends | 15 |
| The Flowers of Russia's Lonesome Steppes | 17 |
| Remarkable Morgan Pike, Yup Yup | 19 |
| Autumn – Autumn – Autumn | 21 |
| I Met a Farmer | 23 |
| Wind Bares Us to its Belly | 25 |
| Pyongyang X108799 to Minneapolis | 27 |
| Soft with the New Flux | 29 |
| Brave Kitten | 31 |
| To Jenny:  Mongrel Dogs and Loving Birds of Prey | 33 |
| Good Old Russia | 35 |
| Who Ever Heard of Us? | 37 |
| I Mow Newly Grown Grass Lightly,  Least the Moon Slide Farther Away | 39 |
| Newlyweds Walk Around in Fancy Dress and Bend Things | 41 |
| A True Story | 43 |
| Winter's Hair is Long on My Shoulders | 45 |
| Poet's Advice to the Young Writer He was a Moment Ago | 47 |
| They Rock My Rocks | 49 |
| No Excuse | 53 |
| As I Hang on My Hook | 55 |
| Joy Monged Me and I Monged Her, Too | 57 |
| All the Way RA ("Faster Troop Faster") | 59 |
| When the Sun Rises Triumphant  in the Sky | 66 |

| | |
|---|---|
| The Nakedly Unfit | 68 |
| That Dog-Eared Loneliness | 70 |
| Noise of Windows Unending | 73 |
| The Picnic Park on July 4th | 75 |
| Suburban Tryst | 77 |
| Good Time Passes | 79 |
| Are You Lonely Charles? | 81 |
| Winter's Rutted Faces | 83 |
| War is a Long Time Away | 85 |
| The Bramble-Faced Veteran of Prairie City | 87 |
| I Pacific Lake in Curiosity's Belly Soft | 89 |
| No Normal-Boweled Persons | 91 |
| Summer Strides with Modesty's Hat | 93 |
| The Memory Trees | 95 |
| My Friend's Fine-Feathering Damsel | 97 |
| Attention: And be a Man | 105 |
| Sky, Trees, and Clouds Passing | 107 |

♦

## *A Moment of Sky!*

Pausing to see a moment of cloudy sky
  on treetops
  crowing at its steely voice,
  olive green warblers pitch dissolving
    variegating sheaths of milky light.
Walking with wind's silent swooping
  whistles when March cajoles
  oaks wrinkled bristling from winter's sharp wit.
Calico leaves hopscotch over marled skin,
  swamp milkweed rustles in trending
  ancient breezes passing, as is the sky,
  as springtime,
    as am I.

◆

# *Inside Wally's Wagon Wheel*
# *(A Small Café)*

Farmers from bowling in the town,
> pins ringing in fluted ears,
> tomorrow's dawn rising in fleeced eyes.

Youngsters unfarmed from a fast car
> approach the counter and cluttered booths
> cavorting before their flight into the night.

An older bowler turns: "My days come to order…"
> bangs her fist on cream doughnuts
> spilling coffee in a hurrying puddle.

"…and not slip past me while he…
> …turns juvenile tittle-tattle to any mother's earth lament,
> watching trees blowing in the crossfire.

My days lay long on your battlefield and pastures
> unceasing when I breathe in all their corners.

Clouds cover this earth floating away but not my son
> while he passes to the next soul on the valley path.

My day loafs with me and we'll see
> your young years never quit these Wheel-parts
> fondly nestling in our arms and never leave the light.

Rapt in people all around his blasted green-piped haze,
> Sonny stands flat in sparrow legs and wings sprouting
> wounded sounds rising from the battlefront."

♦

## Mercantile Solace

Darkness is barred from this place
        honeymooned in decency and commerce.
Wind and snow clash here furious,
        shrill in the paid-for bleach of mercantile row.
Hardly lustrous behind storefront bars, gem cutters magnified eyes bend
        in the dead of night preening diamond light
        and dressmakers' windows suspend mannequin spies.
Shoppers to their dreamtime jewels sparkling,
        heads in clouds of glass counters.
Security guards spin stools at the musical café,
        even thieves take comfort elsewhere.
Crimson buyers on ice in this cockcrow drift –
        swanky dawn sheets sealed by snow,
        village, town, city, the earth is emptied.
Paths in white repose now unmarked, unmanned
        in the solace of mercantile row.

♦

# Life's Most Recent Day is a Picnic with Friends

A searing sun waffle-marks the emerald waters.

Green hills crouch around us and bluffs appear to levitate

    and flirting birds feather-bits spin into reeds.

Picnicking in burnished autumn, basking on grassy banks,

    our bodies unlace, knowing more motions

        than the near and rapid water.

Friends alfresco in the meadow spawning like rainbow trout,

    neither for politeness, not for cities or dynasties past

        and people or the next life,

    opening a pure space to drive Nebraska through –

        the whole creation a picnic without regrets.

Our bodies fuse, our eyes go fishing,

    nothing missed by central headquarters,

    chums couched in copper skylights

        sunning us while the river shimmers nearer and nearer.

♦

# *The Flowers of Russia's Lonesome Steppes*

Pasque wind flowers and sagebrush
      root behind an abandoned house,
Which Amelia pots on my writing table
      to adorn the upper floors of our squat.
Holding a brass bowl of pistachios, she says: "Five
      out of mind Russian brothers
      claim the lower quarters as their billet!
One is priestly, two are drunkards, one just died
      and I never saw the other one.

They have beards and veins in their hands.

Sometimes they lay on the derelict lawn
      like seals eating chipolatas and grits
      and call to each other
      in deep-sounding Russian."

We listen to them, Amelia and me,
      porch-talking on their Siberian night.
A visiting lady (Marion) of the Afterhours Club
      tells us Russians do foul things to children.
      (Eat them, etcetera.)
The fifth brother appears in a window
      blinking his Cossack eyes.

*The Flowers of Russia's Lonesome Steppes*

If they ate anyone, I didn't see them.

As the weeks roll by
> we all pot Steppe-yellow flowers together
> exchanging fondly dubious gestures
> tongued in gay abandon
> without a scrap of flesh shed.

If that is what you call mad,
> I'll be Russian any day.

♦

# Remarkable Morgan Pike, Yup Yup

Remarkable Morgan Pike, yup yup
    flashing with angular ears
    alongside the angling waterways
    fish-tale rivers, wonder castles concealed ashes,
        streams of sunfish family teaming to out-fish him
        and his bluegill-platter hearing.
Mumbling at town square mockery, Morgan Pike,
    his fly casting shadow soars into sky-quilted feathering
    emptying on every corner of rain
    over all the bacon breath and barbiturate talking
        over-easy tables, memories whirling in elbowed grace
    like a five-fingered hawk waiting, yup yup
        for sin, transgressing and leniency on the reel,
        on the oyster mustard back of any old bartender
        who curses lying eyes in frozen faces
    pulsing under broken ice among the ovaries
        gill-breathing life in a bucket.
Smiling upwards now, out of the mirror mirage fish pools
    bringing to mind the purple hues of the Eagles Nest saloon
    streaming from the stools out front where regulars sit
    yup, yupping, mounting channels of air from inside scales
        lifted from the line-intoxicating sun.

♦

## Autumn — Autumn — Autumn

Fall friendly
    clouds idling on the wind,
Basswoods about their tall business,
    hazels barking with feted song or jawing
    in their leafy pockets for safekeeping.
Heavy dew of skies appeasing night striding mysteries
    revel in free play with the world's sap
    abiding in woodland foliage watercolor,
    the bald and scraping moon forest
    suckled by tilt and axis
        rotating the tops of trees.

◆

# I Met a Farmer

I met a farmer who sees rose blood light
      from the moon
           landing in her corn;
It shines up bleeding knuckles, too.
When she jumps off the tractor to touch
           it floats away.
She watches while her wellborn hands grow cold
      and colder until one climbs in her pocket
           while the other explores galaxies of midnight feasts.

♦

# Wind Bares Us to its Belly

A bright night hurls folklores at the earth
    like gyrating voices over us.
We lay on forest stems hungry veins
    or is it bronze leaves from old bones?
The lake is full of unborn seeds and trembling eggs
    ready to burst through currents
        as the icecap burst a week ago
        and sucked back pieces of its edges
        straggling in the slaughter shrouded on shore.
This day shimmering black and blue flotsam flowed
    unstoppable panting webs of time and sand
        warming and chilling by turns
        daylong and nightly
            through us
        over curb-laced street lamps and hot cars
        across tongues intact and garden nettles,
            distended clothesline garments like incandescent skulls
        flapping on the burnt sky.
Rumbling draughts draped limbs and purple hearts hallowed meadows,
    shy breath to dreams hurly in memory's blast
Bare us to its belly.
Laying on each other's bent weight
    our limbs like boughs beyond their reach
    stirring the strength from the inside out.

## Wind Bares Us to its Belly

Is she a mirage of earth's charcoal shaded lungs bawling,
    painted white by the moon to fool me
    or the sense to see beyond the wind
     a replica of her basic goodness?
When we touch
    like earth and its sky
    green stone moss ebbing to its blue bell,
    even little bud things exploding in the air
        to water-still silver bloodlines,
    I say to myself
        this is it
            I love her.

♦

# *Pyongyang X108799 to Minneapolis*

Clouds massing, arching over the city's hearth.

Big blue eyes and leafy lungs shouting:

"Welcome the exile."

"Long live the King!"

"Long live Rock 'n Roll!"

"Long live human rights X108799!"

"Tend him to the chickens, two in every pot!"

"Best chickens to North Korea and damn the pot!"

"Ninth and Hennepin, elders and animals

    this way please!"

"Ever see hermit kingdom captives

    black with flies

        crawling on their taste buds pressed to the ground?"

"No, but I'd rather watch us pray than decay."

"Where is the spring in Pyongyang's gaping keyhole?"

"Where are the flowers and when are the sun's eyes swollen?"

"Only, fellow hermits, when our clouds part company

    in meek and humble pie

        to see the space between lines."

"Welcome PX to Minneapolis."

♦

# Soft with the New Flux

Softening like a baby's nostril unfurling air
    or unfolding colt at dawn
    resting on these loins for-now
    soothing earth roots
    and lineages ride hollow bones.
Sun in April and sea nights chilly,
    chaste clouds drying hillside faces
    and valley heights tumbling to the bottom of sky
    into fresh fault lines – the spider's meal ajar.


Softening with grey furrowing in ancestors sheathed
    inner landscapes to match worldly warming
    or the heat of gravity yelling with fruitful light
    and a shiftiness in tender soles
    treading softly to arcane byways awaiting
    the dawn's oriental charity.


The pores in pine bark and moles eyes waking
    beyond low voices: "Embrace our children
    and hold them to your breast."
A firstborn migrates imprinting mothers' gifts,
    the multiverse likewise in flux
    fusing our ripe chambers with breath companions.

## Soft with the New Flux

Even as the cack-handed chef
    blights the backs of eyes
    turning scriptures brown
    beneath dormant pans,
We walk on gingerly in the soft new flux.

◆

# Brave Kitten

Brave kitten with your calico crouch
      stealthily flaunting wind-tossed hemlock
Spying the eye-riding carriage of just desserts
      through thicket and accruing instincts
      telescopic vertebrae touch retouch re-spot
Pouncing ginger-shell into a dreamy pond shadow
      puffing up the still mirroring lilies
      while sun drools in your monastery drying
Through purging idols in mellow space filled bounty

♦

# To Jenny:
## Mongrel Dogs and Loving Birds of Prey

Sprinting crossbreeds thumping pads
    on the seaside steps of their spines
    polish rain in the Spoon River Valley
    where sun conserves mossy haunts,
        pooches of varying lengths, daisy-powdered paws
        silently bury treasures to favor grace.
Is this why your garden grows crooked madam Jenny?
Will a true to life umbrella shelter your rose-blushed tomatoes?
Yearning Jenny, fuchsia laden, bedding in that violet pinafore
    hoeing through, tasting the beloved garden flora,
    stalking ragged spears for Asparagus Beetles.
Red-tailed hawks and screech owls play to her green-fingered dawdling
    delving in the wheeling wheeling sound cased nosing
    sunken down on her belly inhaling the ground
        a tranquil shield rainbow-like,
    reveling in garden chorales,
To Jenny's mongrel dogs and loving birds of prey.

♦

# Good Old Russia

I

Russia! Great greenish Russia with carbonated teeth.
Sons and daughters of long-haired vagabonds!
      Bounding petulant fiercely hardheaded.
Attack! Night riders and snuff her lanterns.
      Unhorse them and twist their pewter!
Russia Russia with thumbs that scare republics
      sacred blind eyes and picking her nose bloody.
Russia ready to nuclearize everyone and pour oil in our neon.
STOP Russia! Stop all tyrants to find their nosey meat embedded
      or burn them to their core now?
      Line them up and plow them under (Russia the ogre)?
(Russia who laughed while we prayed at Valley Forge
      and roared while we prayed elsewhere since then.)
Russia the wrathful sloth.
GODLESS Russia.
Russia who does not play baseball.

II

March, in many-eyed legions.
Drill in parks, grow in rows and march in parks.
Shout at the clouds and make newspaper hats.
Arm the shirkers, spikes on their elbows
      knives on their knees.

*Good Old Russia*

Call back the veterans, put them together again
      behind Humpty Dumpty's wall.
Renew her four grizzled chambers and head settings
      along byways, fairways, and every which way.
Repaint shadowy buildings bright orange and lay in wait.
Rest and wait for Russia.
Rest and wait.

♦

# Who Ever Heard of Us?

Nobody's ever heard of Gilliland and me.

We watch from high places.

I know his moods and his fancies as he knows mine.

We stroll in crowded smells of milking and tobacco

    saying hello to all our each other's

    and when worse comes from best

    he loans me his woolly vest

    or his diploma or his German motorcycle.

Nobody's ever heard of Gilliland and me.

We pray together and when you hear clapping

    in the church or dulcet whistle tones mid-high in a tree

    at dawn, you know it's us

        teaching voice to the birds,

Him and me.

♦

# I Mow Newly Grown Grass Lightly, Least the Moon Slide Farther Away

The blades in my garden are smiling,
    aurora sky shimmering leaves
    in synch, naked, rising stems fresh behind me
    each bespoke in willowy clumps
    rooster-tailed by reeling cutters
    and fishes' noises at the water lilies.
Friendly oaks aim their elbows at the blind edges
    fraying and canon vocals catch in a knot's eye:
    "Not so close!"
Blue jays gaily-driven on springboard limbs
    dawn squawking in Polish this time? "Breathe easy."
Trim mower trim while the earth moves
    and the moon sulks in a pocket of orbit
    unfurling all mowings and goings in crimson-dappled paths
    criss-crossed in black birds iridescent blue and green
    on one side, speckled with smiles of owls stocktaking.
I see houses around, standing,
    and watch the blades at their best last breath
        of stems moist upward sparkle
            under branching elm and cherry.
The grass that I mow in this night's red and yellow light.

♦

# Newlyweds Walk Around in Fancy Dress and Bend Things

Life feels like wilting flowers
    until moments of fun.
Once a lover eased selfish hours.
Hilltop grass spotted us
    and we dried in the sun.

                red knuckles glowed under our
                            gloves
                            &
                as if to boil ourselves in wedlock
                            &
                as if matrimony is boned on past joy
                            &
                rounded meals from scraps of smiles
                            &
                eating in silence as we pace it isn't the bending
                            &
                vows to regret, it's a lack of space

Then in a lucidly mad-stung sphere
    of yellow spires and dew spots
We start a pot of semen.
One day after work
    a glorious plant spouts.

♦

# A True Story

They aren't putting town names
> on the bottom of Coke bottles anymore.

(Elaine thinks she's pregnant by Phil.)

"Demons are cooking out to split Phil's head," she says,
> "and the left-sided one, the expert, calls him 'Smokey the Bear' while on his right side, the faithful one, keeps saying 'Fearless, fearless' and the demon at the top pecks into his skull like a Red-headed woodpecker."

Phil and Elaine stoke chestnut embers to brainstorm,
> nibbling violets in their hometown, Cokeville Wyoming, where he worked eight months with only seven days' off until he found a Lancaster South Caroline bottle,
>> bringing his total to 1,254 town names.

Elaine is the only one who witnessed Phil's discovery.

♦

## Winter's Hair is Long on My Shoulders

Winter's hair is long on my shoulders.
Melting snow sucks warmth from smoky dawn prairie
        encrusted over solemn grasses still purring.
(A day of hillsong, a meadow bed, and dust demisting
        the dry sky.)
Snow geese in winter's mourning waters,
        gabby stalkers decoys spread with whisky breath
        skyfalls of white feathers bloodied
        while high-flyers jumped the guns to Mexican safe havens
        and so promising of spring.
So much the summer in honeysuckle scarves
        and so promising that russet autumn.

♦

# *Poet's Advice to the Young Writer He was a Moment Ago*

Gotta be tuned in man, see?

Hmmmmm...Busman's holiday of a poem.

That isn't much of a poem is it.

Oh, but who cares if it's unread, they'll buy it after I'm famous.

Famous?? Who wants to be famous. I want to be a river

      swimming in the currents, for I like to swim

      and teach the fish comforting words,

      float on my back in the sun and visit the sea.

Advice, don't forget the advice.

Gotta be tuned in, lemme see

      advice: hmmmmm – specifics…using words to name things

      all the while listening at my world's mouth

      damp on my glasses and a crick in vocabulary.

Which world? What if my world loses its choice of words to mouth?

Bend one of the ears

      or better yet unlock an eye and let grammar be the mouth.

I might get arrested by the heartbeat of a poem.

Yeah, or smell fishiness in matter-of-fact passages

      or learn how syntax or imagery gestate.

Then can I be a doctor poet, like uh…Doctor Uh…

Or a garden poet with rakish syllables vibrating

      and poe about the way sun lights the dew

      in my lawn as I mow new spring grass.

*Poet's Advice to the Young Writer He was a Moment Ago*

Then, I'd be a gardener poet, wouldn't I?
Or a gardener without deadheading or pruning
      or a poet without inner landscaping
      never finished just abandoned:
      the trembling flesh of next season's writing.
Oh yeah? Well, I might be just a poet
      ironing my brown checkerboard pants
     phrasing words in my shrinking head
          until the bells tone and start to peal.
Yes, disarming off-kilter images ripening under the plot
              incubating verse,
         my tongue in its mouth-seizing voice
     unearthing how the poem looks and sounds
        'til everything shines more brightly than before.

♦

## *They Rock My Rocks*

I ask two kids with liquid noses to be quiet.
They retreat to a hideaway, then, return as if repossessed
    alongside an adult.
Vaseline or such like clings to her hair framing a puce-flare face,
    hands withdrawn into her sleeves:
"My children are free!" she shouts.
"They are loud, too loud," I reply, "for a combat soldier waving a
pencil and pad:
    these are my writing rocks and you didn't place them
        like those red spiders clutching your bosom.
    So please leave my poor timeless rocks alone."
They step backwards as violet sky murmurs
    and I hear machine valves grating.
Antlers shred clouds and one foot pounding is her other half:
    "What'd call my Elaina Marie and do to my kids
        the spawn and best part of our insides?"
"Get off my rocks, please," I snapped. "Every second counts:
    I'm trying to write a poetic drama on this rock bed."
"You're crazy, some goddamn nut atheist breadloser
    you'd leave bacon to starve in the rain
    when it's crying for ribs to cling to."
The behemoth raises a granite stone, to toss
    watching as it heaves itself and smashes

      his right foot into fossil tracks across quirky primal faces.
"A green warrior recycling, I write to find quiet in a lagoon of stars
          rattled, wincing at our shuffling pride."
"She says you're wounded too, crazy with bad things."
Family funnel inside him, huddling, trotting away.
I say, "These fossils touch you from their dusty entrails!"
The sun climbs in its sky and the rocks grow warm,
      birds ho-humming, pistol-noises and china plates,
      assault cars, bridges, radios shuddering,
      gavels and benches, errant pigeons, judges
      cudgels pliant and war room shutters
      drumming cadence to field mortuaries
      felling trees and water grinding to glass.
Bombs tick-tocking with napalm, cymbals and thunderclaps rolling,
      Humvees screaming armor and dog grinding teeth,
      rubber elastic bands, snowmaking and atoms,
      atoms atomizing, nuclei sizzling, particles particularizing.
Pressure builds until plate tectonics unfold
      "…and then a ligature," shouts the returning Leviathan.
      In rotting socks a comrade of that family snaps
          the inhaling off from his brother's inbreath.
Extraterrestrial star-shells rocking each other's arms
      off the rails exploding these rocks

and when the dust and bedbugs clear

    miniscule powder lays thick on abandoned veins.

We occupy the same obit into shared eyes

    when a writer on rocks dares to question kids with liquid noses

        who play there after all, a corkscrew of spines

            making houses with Dixie Cups

            under an azure flag popping

                gently in the breeze.

◆

# No Excuse

"Excuse me sir, but you're a poet, aren't you?"

"Yes, why else am I standing on my head
> looking at picnicking and randy kids in a public park
>
> with paperback books all around."

"Well, I'm a reporter and..."

"Of course you're a reporter, why else would you excuse me sir."

"Well –"

"What you want to know is how and why, right?"

"Why, why yes; but how do you know?"

"I started as a reporter with the Free Press."

"I want to be a poet – tell me what is takes."

"Husky fingers with a daring turn of yielding brain and a rotor –
> all poets have a rotor somewhere in their brain
>
> husky fingers and a rotor; no, no, just the rotor,
>
> no room for husky fingers messing up the turns of mind."

"Oh, I see."

"I don't know why – as a kid it's been there
> usually in my kidneys. Down here
>
> in my kidneys, which at present
>
> since I am standing on my head are elevated to a height
>
> over my skull and in fact higher
>
> than most vital body parts except my brain."

"Well how'd you do it upright?"

"Husky fingers surrendering to contrary feelings in dialogue doing more than one thing at the same time,

      whereas the rotor in the headgear

      steers between graceful drama, uneven chants

        and cunning idioms of the world's epic chorus."

"I bet I know how they got husky, your fingers."

"Yes," (starting a giggle) "too many trying to be nice poems."

"Aha, haha..." (half-laugh, jaw-locked in chest-weight)...

"Hehe...hehe..." (starting to lose balance)...

      "Oh, oh stop, you're making us laugh...

      hahaha..." (chuckling, tilting, rotoring

      down to the grass, laughing)...

"What the hell's so funny all the time?"

"Our voices jangling with haunted kinships,

      revising secret speeches in burlesque moments

      attending to each other:

        no excuse."

◆

## As I Hang on My Hook

Pull clouds from your sky,
      wear them like a garland
      or seed them
            in your ploughing.

You smile and distance is gone.
Let's laugh again while lonesomeness prowls
      in the blind crowd below.

Skip down the red lane
      sensing your way
            to my tangled vine.

As I hang on my hook,
      hush and pluck me
            as the sun sets.

♦

# *Joy Monged Me and I Monged Her, Too*

JOY MONGER!
    (For Joy monged me) She monged me 'til I walked
        with a limp and my hair stood on end.
Then I monged her some, and more
    and more like roses
        and farmers about a field with planting.
Down the happy red brick streets she monged me.
Joy.
Joy.
Joy.
And monging her I found joy –
    tickling green blades and stars offspring.
    Quasar font of joy alive in human cells
    and gold clock flowing to full
        to full and away.
Round earth bubbling and the moon's trees blanching.
Silent insects calling with imprints now of enigmas past.
Sleep-hollow streets and future bright beams burning
    moonfire and nuclear weather.
And joy,
    Joy and I monging.
Joyfully.

◆

# *All the Way RA ("Faster Troop Faster")*

Regular Army documents signed,
> miles of bumf, combat feet and tons of them
>> ending in a barber's chair
>>> with bad breath.

From the stealthy butcher-barber with body bag breath
> to here and there with hair or no hair
> and gleaming kitchens of rattling
>> equipment
>>> stacked on cemetery shelves.

Pass in a dusty truck with metal squeaks
> to a shovel swinging
> in a hand and marching
> much marching to melodies two/two-time.

Hup/hup/hup/ing down-the-hill
> up-the-hill RA all-the-way RA all-the-way
>> airborne!

Fifty recruits growling and sunrise in the pines; running
> ranks, Caterpillars grooving the battlefield
> ranks running all the way.

Pause for breath and run in ranks.
> Surprise hot food
>> and rifle range, rifle bang
> down-the-hill up-the-hill all-the-way
>> rifle bang RA.

*All the Way RA ("Faster Troop Faster")*

Hosing down the tanks
    (and hosing up the barber with decomposing breath)
    headlights, the long march back,
    troops in tanks for a ride to clean
    the Pattons with water every absolute night.
Barracks and no taps sounding.
    Firelight. Two/two-time
        and hup/hup/hup/hup – faster troop faster.


Jackie is a trooper and she is fast by nature.
    Nothing new as RAs go,
    she obeys orders and prefers to give them.
Jackie joined because she, the only child
    beside her mother's enlarging bosom
    opaque and no doubt about it – pregnant, too,
Feels pushed away, away to Fort Knox
      barracks and this black fogsoft soggy night
      with military asphalt wilting
    her near-bald head and baggy fatigues unstarched
      and still shiny.
How is she? She is always fine but her mother says,
    yeah her mother "…and if I don't do something
    about Jackie's throw-a-brick-and-take-a-lick

*All the Way RA ("Faster Troop Faster")*

    she'll face the judge with infinite lawn and luminous hair,
    then in the hell jail her joy shrivels and falls off."


After chow-long lines by all the phones to moms
    Jackie strides away from the company area.
    (The barracks pals, spitblack boots, new soles
    shining heels past the last billet
    one as good as another, waxed floors, identical doors.)
Penalty squad passes. Hup/hup/hup/hup RA all-the-way –
    "Let's hear it troop!
    Move it out, double TIMMME – HU!"
    Boots double-timing hup/hup past her.


Quiet now, nobody on the roads;
    newness passes and she alone, hands in her pockets
    hands in her pockets and relaxed.
At home, Peggy Sue strokes her belly in the Chenille-trimmed bed
    with the beam of life mothering inside,
    away from the maroon Ford's backseat
    where the recruiter's arm patch comes alive,
    rowing metronomes of the raven's beak-pointing pushiness
    thrusting through his steaming flair.
Remembering him on the thumb she hitchhiked with Jackie
    to enlist face-shining on rain laced roads.

*All the Way RA ("Faster Troop Faster")*

"Trooper!"

    And dare to step on the raven face, smash –

"Trooper goddammit, get your hands out of your pockets."

The insignia glare swiveling: looking for heavy combat voices

    can't hear but somewhere –

"Goddammit…" from the left face

    flag-waving scowls in the night.

"…didn't you hear me?"

"Huh?"

"JesusMotherofMary, I said – GET YOUR HANDS

    OUT OF YOUR POCKETS!"

"Why? Now here, now why, why?"

"Because I told you so."

"Uh?"

"You see this stripe, trooper?"

"Yeah, stripe, yellow v-slashing eye on an arm."

"Then you know to call me: Yes, PFC."

"Okay. Yes, PFC."

"Why do you think you are here?"

"Uh, the raven sent me; the raven sends everyone."

"You're here to take orders, goddammit. Now get your head out of yer ass."

She thinks: head is never adrift of ass. "Okay."

"Ha? What'd you say?

## All the Way RA ("Faster Troop Faster")

Over here, sergeant, YESSIREE bob, come look at this *mother*."
Sergeant approaches, more eyes on Jackie's arms
> looking and slashing – his face like a wrist
> hairy and veined.

Eyes lost in the face, eyes on the arms – potato eyes!

"How's come you got your hands in your pockets, buddy?"

"Alright, my hands are out; put them in your pockets."

"What'd you call me?"

"Nothing, I didn't..."

"SERGEANT, you call me sergeant, boy. Goddammit
> I had me enough bullshit from you contraries
> all day now and night. Take your fucking hands
> out of yer pockets and come with me. MOVE!"

PFC grinning like peeling a banana,
> hostile hard hands grow stiff from his arms.

"Goddamn, troop, I warned you. Now the sergeant
> he don't take no shit from you scaredy-cats; he's busy.
> He's gonna make you busy. Looks like yer goin'
> back to the mess hall."

"But, I..."

"You disobeyin' a direct order: Gimme fifty push-ups –
> Faster troop faster."

*All the Way RA ("Faster Troop Faster")*

Jackie mulls: Shut up PFC, the sergeant comes to bite your secrets.

    The sergeant gives orders.

    The sergeant is the man. He runs the show.

    The PFC takes orders from the sergeant.

    The raven gives orders with brown stripe-eyes

        to the trooper.

"Shut up PFC."

"Yes Sergeant Sir."

"Now, godfubbleduckitydamnyou trooper, come with me –

    what the hup/hup! What the hup/hup/hup you doin'

    on the ground? Diggin' the hole you was born in?

    You can dig a hole in the mess hall.

    Take you twenty years to get out of there."

"Pushups – I was…"

Sergeant walking fast toward Jackie, slaps

    her on the olive drab,

    foot-pushes her towards the mess,

    the one neon strip lit round-the-clock

    and Sundays, too.

To the raven's kitchen and fix food for the green swarming

    head homing contraries to scrub, sleep, eat and scrub

    metrical ticking hup/hup/hup/ing away.

    "I never told you to do no push-ups."

*All the Way RA ("Faster Troop Faster")*

        Then uppity-up and away ahead of the man,
            PFC off to the left,
            the sergeant stops and bellows: "PFC?"
"Yes Sergeant Sir."
"Did you type up the duty roster for tomorrow's KP?"
"Yes Sergeant."


Bolting, Jackie's back to him, sprinting away from the prankster raven
        beyond the earth of mess halls
        with the broken nose cook who poisons cats
        and spits on clean pots and pans,
        down civvy street in the night to the unborn light.
Nobody in tow, PFC gone, sergeant withdrawn,
        everybody departed from the mess halls, orderly rooms
        and emptied beds in the barracks.
For tomorrow, faster troop faster.
Run all the way for the raven's scavenging vow
        furthering for a day to live life anew
        when she dials Peggy Sue:
"This babe is from my bloodshed not your battleground," she shouts
        down the phone to Jackie
        from the freedom dwelling inside
        on balanced wings neither buoyed up
        or weighed down – hup/hup/hup/hup.

♦

# When the Sun Rises Triumphant in the Sky

Downtown buyers cruise dime store candy

    hurrying to places they know

    whispering through small change and coffee.

      A statuesque street artist outdoes his habits

        slashing X's in his mourning mural,

        pirouettes into a truck's grill,

        bouncing bouncing away.

A hawker dressed as a nun selling papers –

    rounded eyes, she phrases words,

    shouts news, listens back,

    as shoppers hit the salons

    meandering in foyers embraced by mirrors.

Mesmerized, main street's shiny mouths unlock.

A mademoiselle with roses in her hair spots sparrows,

    hops in her mother's shadow mimicking

    mannequins' legs bowed like noodles:

"It's an ocean of bows wrapped in pink –

    collect the bows for a Celtic party.

    Dress as a gift or a crab or a cross

    or put a leash on them and they'll walk me."

The crowd thrusts as if light deserted day,

    voices on the morning's bell wake heavy dreams,

    smoked bus flecks massing skin

    windbitten in many-pennied faces and hands wrought.

# *The Nakedly Unfit*

The nakedly unfit forever evangelizing.
For piety's forsaken eyes alone
    on naves prostrate gestures,
    clerical collars cradled in sandstorms,
    amorous robes from sacred bones,
    penises rouse like sinking stones.
Autumn sky wails far from blush cheeks bedding for mercy's sake,
    windswept over mourners' new marrow.
    Stride out against fits of paradise
    upon flocks white lower parts
    and billowy ecclesiastic bellies
While inside sing the passion honestly for pilgrims' toil,
    believers breathing merrily upon their sermons
    searching heartily for faith,
    invited to face loosely crossed music,
    kneeling at cassocks opening and arms blessed lifting.


Level preachers' chancels – Drop their kneecaps in water basins.


To winter then for moods cloistered pretty faces
    to sun sacred princes traveling apart,
    blood goblet chants from bald brows and primal instinct
    breathe as stiff as gilded breastplates
    on the folded wings of holy spirits.

# That Dog-Eared Loneliness

The loneliness which comes after a quarrel
When each discovers their ancient self
Leaves us again in a basket of snakely arms.

No entertainment or well-loved crowd,
      no cherished ball game or blades of grass,
          or lambs oblique hopping or the sun's aging trees,
Can ease that dog-eared loneliness.

The fear of that self is vague time
Soon to be fog until we meet each other's
Paths unbound from snakely arms.

◆

## Noise of Windows Unending

Are you startled by sonic trails whitening pale skies
      over glacial freeze forceps and savanna sweat
      or voices of lost boys inside volcanoes and ocean grottoes,
      corn dusted blue tractors manuring,
      or waltzing cheerily to sweet commerce
      through the windows we adore?
Have we never stumbled before these days packaged to self-serve?
Let the chewed up noise recoiling in our heads
      wild and unimaginable thoughts
      pass through reflecting windows,
      tunnel through our entrails
      and flush the black drizzle of a weeping world.

◆

# The Picnic Park on July 4th

In this public place of corncobs and beef wheat
      the rain lush laughing grass
      unfinished bricks of bandstand wall and rickety shelter,
Americans are mighty good and hungry!
Feeding around tables red and white checkered with cutlery spent
      stabbing flightless poultry,
          Independence Day roosters shrieking,
          feathered reservists daft panic in pink petunias
          crying against a wall of blood.
An ocean of tongues lashing and ear shots nosing eye lit heads.
A son is born to light,
      born out of the past and squeezed capillaries.
Four babes thumb sucking through dummies for safety's sake
      point to a dog's jaw propped open with chicken drumsticks.
A child held to the heavens bawling
      angles in the sun's backhanded stare
      above the feasting dancers.
Dappled ballerinas tearing at their ribs
      biting the heads off turtle sweets, in orange teeth.
A lady strips an oak's ash-grey bark
      pounding it to skin clinging cloth.
Two men roar and bite each other's ears
      and the day moon beds in pastel clouding.

*The Picnic Park on July 4th*

Groundsmen eating from earth, batter its roots and leaves.
Matriarchs tease the trickle from plants
    waxing it on their thighs.
Elders wise-ways wear mountainsides in their loins.
Patchers fix holes in the water runs
    clipping their pale teeth to the neck of the emptying basins.
Dancers spin around their shadows
    barreling backwards into a foxhole.
Wild lights flash across a face and its cracks.
A muffled teen baulks at her first goose skull
    and eats from among the bones.
Seamen with tattoos on their necks
    bellow in their groins
    jumping on flowers and rooting them dry.
Two shackled nephews twist around a table
    eating their grandfather's duck.
A Latino miss shines glasses on the sky's fiery lips.
The dancers wheel and curve and creak and lapse
    skirting their orbits
    while fire snaps at the goats tethering bush.
All the while shouts, grunts, and serrated hammers
    beat dry lifeless birds blistered on a grill
    while global stars above the fruited plain
    draw daylight from amber waves of grain.

♦

## Suburban Tryst

Three children with placards ask me for candies
      when a fourth, vexed, appears like a prayer
      from the beseeching hollow above his breeches.
"Look, my pockets are empty of sweets,"
      and snapping the cord of my rosary
      sifting coral prayer beads into each palm:
"There, 27 each to string and pray."
Off they skip with gay abandon
      ditching their signs in tall weeds,
      singing: 'Sweets for my Sweet, Sugar for my Honey,
      Please Give Candy Instead of Money!'

♦

# Good Time Passes

Sweet potato leaves and joy in the air.

Spiked sky brushing damp earth.

Down the hill to the water

    swashing rattle, clods tumbling

    and land seep crusty cores unfurling.

II

Grass is waving,

    sun foaming in the dunes,

    branch crossed clouds on river skin

    and moss is moss.

Sycamores' floating leaves wiped with a splash.

Pounding feet track in the mud.

III

Glitter in canopies dreamland gifts,

    spider webs glistening lime and avocado rays

    drawn to earth's thirsty bodies,

    downwind sounds and water-mussed

Noises of human beings quiet lying.

IV

Roots still grounded,

    fruit on feral limbs,

    air ripples on the water.

Chill, and those of a view look beyond mist to see.

♦

## Are You Lonely Charles?

Do you hear the wind's waning edge?

Does your amber sky feel empty?

Do you listen to households quiet in their shady skirts?

How does the crescent moon touch you?

Is it too long 'til sunrise?

Do you find the hawks slashing beaks uplifting?

Does a miasma of gossiping faces unnerve you?

Did the stars burn holes in you that night?

How does a clenched voice set your blood against you?

What makes you scrape nails across your ruby eyes?

Why did you smash that mirror over your knee?

And what makes you bite yourself?

Are the answers to hang for
      over your springboard nursery chair
        stifling the neck's spinning tongue?

♦

# Winter's Rutted Faces

Winter's rutted faces
    between lush cheeks and fairy-tale conceits
    far and wide through flesh and native refrains
    halt in jokers circling lengths.
Love's limbs fragile leaning towards the spring
    bow to earth's titanic rocking
    headlands in pancake camouflage
    brooding like a poem abandoned.

♦

# War is a Long Time Away

(Sitting in an army latrine, talking with Private Schott,
    a shaved head waiting to be discharged.
    I am waiting to be discharged for another reason.)

Schott: "Hey, you waitin' for discharge?"

"Yeah."

"What kind?"

"219."

"Why?"

"I'm a pacifist."

"A what?"

"I don't believe in war."

"Hey, how'd juh get in the Army then?"

"That's a long story."

"Must be crazy."

"What?"

"You must be crazy, man; anybody knows you gotta have wars."

"Why?"

"Dats the way it is, man. Why? Is it against
    yer religion or sompun?"

"You could say that."

"Man, must be a screwed-up religion; that's all I got
    to say: must be a screwed-up religion."

♦

# The Bramble-Faced Veteran of Prairie City

Why do they lean back and laugh?
        And how often?
Why isn't grass *really* green
        and why is their Sunday toiled so quietly?
(Distant sounds like baroque opera)
All because this native son
        bleeds from wire barbs and booby trap eyes
While they wind their watches?

◆

# I Pacific Lake in Curiosity's Belly Soft

I Pacific Lake in curiosity's belly soft
And fill and frills and hills of waters reddening seeds
Elasticated and probe-eyed hipsters' plastic dressings
      (I feel a forgiving all-day longing)
Our wellborn and groove tongued algae ahead of time

City blessings from lilies yellow wet stems opening
And all the eras' fare-thee-wells coast gassing along
Oil toxins marinated ripening flesh on dining tongues
Trembling with the edgy crusts of continental drift
Smearing herbicides in gut flesh and boneheaded blessings
From Pacific Lake to the Great Barrier Reef

◆

## *No Normal-Boweled Persons*

During a midday forage
    beyond our recycled Burma Shave second marker
Extending the track
    linking our settlement to the salt:

At one end of the temple, slot mouth clocking machines,
    food piled at the center,
    trolley pickers peeling rows of foodstuffs.
    No normal-boweled person dreams
    of matching its canned purity,
        awing at caged eggs weighed and counted
        in a census more accurate than our clan's –
Toothpaste power brushes whiten teeth unbleached
    even after death and after that
        for good.
Green watermelon drums vigor-boom,
    redness of skinned meat in broods,
    shavers sit like pocket vegans
    waiting to face graze or optionally deroot
    or grow any pattern in instalments.

The loudest noise is music from liquor aisles,
    brass parts clinking,
    paper fans rustling

   in synthetic waters purring hotly.
Feigning fish offers and phoney facial guarantees
Near the circular appliance department
   in ropes of sham pearls clunking:
      washing machines

      toasters

      knife sharpeners

      eyebrow pluckers

      etcetera electric.
Gear wheeling clocks chime odd hours,
   deodorant coupons are pocketed with lottery tickets.


Dolls born in advance states of feeding,
   far from static parades and barrel rolls,
   adept at lying and winking speak: "10 bucks"
   to bid on price for Chinese faults at the checkout.


Now offering foraging grounds at our settlement,
Normal-boweled persons cross the Burma Shave second marker
   tempted by signboards for living garlic,
   mushroom and wild mustard burgers,
Dissatisfied with packaging, stomach remedies,
   and world-weary TV dinners,
Disgruntled by the reasons they accepted tons of wounded flesh.

♦

## Summer Strides with Modesty's Hat

Summer trails her brown curls
        across green, yellow, and red grassed prairies
Never forgetting her prolonged caresses
        singing to Wounded Knee's crying eyes.
What is better than skylarks at larking to ease their pain
        or is partings mistake always today's face?

Summer, polished and prone in her diamond-fingered calling,
        save the Lakota people's lyrical grasslands,
        her modest plea to surrender genocide half-released,
Rupturing earth's bruised soul rapt in tribal ancestry.

Summer in her air blue shroud,
        secrets spaced in the Badlands vine
        dialling up sisterly Madonnas from her capped spine,
Residing like a jagged light wading in a warrior's smile
        she tips her hat for awhile.

Federal agents in a bar, rebel furnace mouthed and ingot eyeballs
        hotly ill-disposed to Summer's striding
        wince at her double-jointed handshake.
Who is soft or lost with pain or racked with slaying
        too fixed to rest under modesty's hat?
Next, their clickety steel heels prance into the raucous winds.

*Summer Strides with Modesty's Hat*

Summer, her ivory eye sees everything as awake,
    whimsters, pyramid sharks, cost cutters
      or sudden gleams from sea life to canyon strife
    to birth with all manner of lazybones and chieftains,
Striving to unheard drumbeats of native song.

♦

# *The Memory Trees*

High in my latticed tit-for-tat sycamore
      swimming in currents of leaves
         pulsing veins
      overlapping branches unending.
Spring striving yellow whirls of wind
      fused roots elastic watching
      gardens garlic smells wildly
Breathe in and above the earth turning.
White oaks sway juiced in exquisite sky orbs.
Copper faced surgeons rapt nervous flux
      and blood sheets patched openings
Beckoning like mariners recalling the Pacific shelters
      names of the sunken past now sailing leeward.
A vortex darts after itself stirring mountain ash
      balding in flesh laced mothers and flowering streams.
Countless tide bidding flags fling the moon's waves
      and seal churning of white teeth orbs.
White mist and slippery elm and trees gone by lay watching
      seasonal guests disperse hackberry fruiting
         while the roundness of rocks float on water
            and fire combs these bluffs.
Grown up trees woven in ant song and the ants spark
      fresh lifespan rising from seed through decay.
(Oh, to be in one spot at a time under sky fire rushed off its feet.

## The Memory Trees

Riding the wind's generous breath and water coursing to its roots.)
Another day neither here nor there
      in this or that ornamenting scotch pine,
      yonder grooved sugar maple aging grey,
          brown barked saplings singing heroes,
              soldiers of wars bearing flags we pledged
      along purplish fields and bright green foliage reviving.
No nails in our shadows yet from unborn pride.
Praying beyond the sun, tomfoolery learned and unlearned.
Hands all aglow in laughing souls, seahorse eyes and singing on buses.
Secret growling orbs hang godly with no jangly speed needed
      by any of the candle burning memory trees.

♦

## *My Friend's Fine-Feathering Damsel*

How she goes humming in the night's choral mulch
      drinking the murky milk of thinly spaced discords,
      loose doggerel lungs running hooves on earth's casings,
Coursing beyond abiding breeze.
Streams shine her green-eyed mirror
      tolling silent, beckoning a daybreak beacon.


When I first met Dee
      at her painting studio
      I thought: she's sitting
      right in front of me:
Glancing, her image caught and mingled
      beyond knitted shades of ornate braids.
I was ready to show her my Eveready torchlight
      on the canvas of hydrangeas climbing free
      but two grasping pilgrims flitted to her
          attending to their prize
      like bats coming home from a recce
          in Mexico.


Sweet leaves and joy veil in silken air.
Spiked sky brushing damp earth,
      honeysuckle waves pushy with purple finch warbling,
      sea particles foam horsing through her belly

## My Friend's Fine-Feathering Damsel

And mass is mass rooting each other's golden dreams.

Days short-lived often for too little trying
      thirsting in arched backs and delicate lips.
Do we live without the sweat of a fishmonger's hidings
      singing to simpler desires?
Do we live on childhood residues
      and smiling white clouds reborn
      again, in renewing grasses?
Are these nights long airing holes piercing the astral roof
      the same as the moon lit from our eyes?

My troublemaker mind passes like prayers
      wedding a basic goodness of all ages
      if you like,
Wishing our spring lovely well
      before timeless antiquity's underbrush absorbs us
      in her peacock-feathered hat,
          like barbed fleece shrinking
            to untangle wanton laments lame as wool.

Why do we tie ourselves to each other?
      Do railroad trains and cash registers cease,
        onlookers at the kiosk turn into papier-mâché,
        traffic, vaulting swans, police freeze in their tracks,

## My Friend's Fine-Feathering Damsel

Catholics sit crossed, Anglicans firmly clutch
property deals and kneel deferring to holy eons past,
and pink-faced time stops its tick at our emporiums?

Mental wars continue, and what besides 84,000
    acts of my own thickset design have I done
    to end my own cranial drifting? (Or could I do?)
    Could hate less (have hated)
    Could love more (do love)
        should work harder (am working, obviously)
        effort plus what – from the Farmers' Almanac?

Silent alchemy far behind her teeth
        through windows
        up red-nippled backstreets
    she forges a cloud and the hustlers fall asleep
        while others lift their veils and weep.

Cloudlets weave and curdle in chambers
    stillness cracked fissures
        seeing through fossil eyespots.
Hovering wind sighs for a last nourishing breath
    of clock carrying rivals
        cooking schemes to spoil her with new-fangled salaries –
Only to find that she unfuses secrets from the backs of their eyes

## My Friend's Fine-Feathering Damsel

   turning laughter a yellowish purple –
All the while a dripping
  and a halt
    coming
  a halt coming when form
  begets form, even as past
  and present-days walk away (from us)
    even in death.


Where does she go on a night like this
  when wind scales on ice
    and sky turns
      pearly whirly
        into itself and finally
Rewinds?
Trees, restless, hunt the angular jaws at daybreak.
Long gone frogs stare frozen at stars violet foliage
  and my friend tries to sleep in his head's rusty hut.


Fossils wearing boulders stone trousers
  rock and bone, wear and tear, erode, renew
   *light light*
  too soft to explode
  but eating like the softness left
  in a baby's nostrils or a still colt's breath at dawn.

## My Friend's Fine-Feathering Damsel

My friend's fine-feathering damsel
    turns garden beds into lilac rows
    while we are easy to bury ourselves in thickening hearts,
        a formula to match the sun's bone-jarring heat
        or gravity hot with no light,
    only succeeding with patient warriors' feet
        and boxed plots waiting for new seed.

He dreamt of Dee one day, the energy
    of her power residing in him.
At first, her warmth alone outward and away
    encircling orange and black monarch wings,
    summer solstice bitten in cupped palms
    as solitary grace is plated in quivering storm folds.

Where does she go on a night like this
    to leave him with his cherishing
    at the river, to touch and see?
In that presence: the feeling of her breath,
    blue grass under toes,
    star machine in her evening elbowing
    across waning moons green and silver dares,
    cool sparks multiplying inside our minds.

*My Friend's Fine-Feathering Damsel*

But now, what of the long years
    ahead?
Even now, seeing him as a growing father
    or the juxtaposition of one
    he falls from her grace without a shadow
    of doubt to bear his weight.
What are we to do? Build houses
    filled with knicky-knacky children
    and well-being?
Will their youngsters be mislaid in televised slew,
    chase each other naked through its callous turning drama,
    sit up with dusty rabbits coughing into soapy mornings
        sun rising in pubescent faces?
Will our children entomb us and buy a plot on Mars
    or donate our dregs to indigenous peoples
        for compost with broken treaties
    legally and with clothing and nudity/crudity bookends?
Are there three eras in the future
    when we'll each remember
    playing hopscotch in her parent's garage
    while they shop for new pistols at Wilkins' Market?
In one another's absence, will there be ages of ill-spreading gut
    withdrawing oars on quiet afternoons,
    Che Guevara T-shirts or pleasant married years
    striving to wake up one lifetime

## My Friend's Fine-Feathering Damsel

or another to each other's gracious smiles?
Will she still read to him
    and one night wake thinking
    of the guy who grinned at her
        loving?
The next morning would they be in a better mood,
    better than they had been, once in a while?
Might my friend be pleased if somewhat puzzled?
Perhaps, she might go to the library twice
    in a week, but won't know why.
After the second visit, she might notice a new mole
    on his white freckled belly.

Years will pass like armored ducks in a row
    and he may dream of the military a few times.
Once, leaving the Rib Shack after dinner
    (the spring night is warm
    and she is drowsy) a bicycling lady
    passes along the sidewalk, shouting:
    "I smell sweaty socks and tremble
        at rose-colored loins as they've never trembled before."

For now, as I pass their room, his head on her chest,
    left arm around her golden eagle tattoo:
    she feathers him, a fine foal in rising dew,
    caressing his effigy of her.

When you ask me in broad daylight if I am bound to love people
    just like that: I'll smile and say
        "I always have"
And life begins again.

♦

## *Attention: And be a Man*

Throw down your grommets
      from the enflamed slacks of flag day
      standing in short-lived formation.
Bandit noised red trapped knuckles saluting
      ant-faced green drumming cadences
      jingling loose change in massed pockets.
Strive homeward to the wolf paw imprints,
      the lizards temperate stutter,
      foremothers' wounded souls.
You are bound to give birth to something,
      pardons for corsairs money-spinning glut
            oozing from molten battle scarred eyes,
      or finding the joy of knowing who you are.

♦

## Sky, Trees, and Clouds Passing

In the clodded garden the onion shields grow
> around the family's ruddy bare feet
> in waxy roots of purple flowers,
> mosquitos buzzing in the sweat of nature's labor
> > they work.

Their leisurely toil is hoeing and spading
> bending fingers to the soil.

They itch in the garden's hide and spend themselves.
Mother with her eagle joints and lighted bulb,
> her eroding cane with four notches,
> leads them singing with pilgrimage eyes
> perusing the eastern edge for crop raiders.

Mother with her calipered leg flattening clods and hoeing
> raises her head for the effect of strength
> pressing against her walker and harness to hoe a line.

Her breath leads the pain from her most sensitive heart.
Now a rainbow passes
> over her and the final family member
> is born and being raised
> in, of all places, the garden.

The mother's daughter casts her eyes flirting with their shadows
> and wields the shears offhand to mount
> rose petal stems leaving V-shapes in flesh barbed
> like sharks' teeth biting her blood pocked arm.

## Sky, Trees, and Clouds Passing

Still, she snips the branches clean,
    no time to bleed or turn her back coyly
    ignoring the pain; once when she did
    her toeprints pierced a piece of cardboard
    which blew away in a summer storm.
At school, she knows sly Mistress Lofty
    seeing with a ringed eye the angular pupils,
    dusty velvet covers of learning and learned,
    downy skinned and thoughts left clustered,
    closeted until fetched to cheer company
        when company sit in the garden
        smell its lemons, the rockery and shrubs
        licking the company with crosstalk.

A child, one of the sons, restless on his heels
    sits watching an ant – the bad ant of the garden –
    grizzled buck ant – the trellis its pocket piece –
    which does its courting under rose-tinted moons
    and in other generations.
The boy's eyes trace the ant field and feel his mother's
    warmth and the galloping hoe sits up
    barking at the ant as his toes kick the metal blade,
    flinging the handle around his head in a figure eight,
    digging fast rows to find Buck and deeper
        finding another ant – a rescue ant with antlers

## Sky, Trees, and Clouds Passing

        and radio pack

            cruising rows spotting broken ants to rescue.

The matted earth crunching ground of the family tilling soil.
      Sentinel leaves and the uppermost foliage,
          fountains in the woody stems echo of water running
              into tips of branches genteel rustling.
Above, spawned red-shouldered hawks flapping in the sky.
Beyond, unseen gasses spine bristling clouds
      flushing across sky and pulling the earth
          foaming with thunder; vapors traipse that space
              owning its bright choral whistling,
                  oceans flow and crack on earth,
Invisible elements felt by these gardeners seeding.
(Bark, bark, the eagle beak,
      its fawnish bathing suit in fly zones
          perforated gravity and forever away, forever
              and away
                  baying nomadic envelopes of gases.)

Bright thunderous firing billowing mass ferment,
      lightening splits cellar doors and blows
          wide open bright canopy eyes to blue light.
The cosmos rasping the heavens clean, torn pockets moist

## Sky, Trees, and Clouds Passing

    glowing and shavings from airspace:
Celestial curling upbeat and inside out
        upside down sky curve clouds firing radiant
            sown in light
        under hoes hands dribbling seeds to the rows.
The whirling upturned firmament to a thousand pieces joined,
        tunneling slants into dark brown soil infused,
        shiny legged ant fields criss-cross cobalt rows
            dodging the boy's hoe.
Limitless forms vanish in elastic columns infinitely colored.

The wind draws the earth rooting trees
        pulling across sky
        levering families.
Watery blush vapor floating and gardeners sensing
        the funnelling forces clouds make
        pulling at the earth and all reforming.
Sky, trees, and clouds passing
        tussling with earth's mothers
        to unending fertile corridors
        tireless growing as the family
            subtly renewing in the garden.

♦

www.ingramcontent.com/pod-product-compliance
Lightning Source LLC
Chambersburg PA
CBHW061334040426
42444CB00011B/2913